Hearts and Souls
The Beginning

By

Bathsheba Dailey

Tracks of Life

A New Beginning
Is Better Than An Old Ending

A Thank You Note

I would like to thank my girls first for just being themselves and showing me that when I feel like I have no one else in my life, I will always have them.

Thank you to Earnest Beckelheimer for always believing in me when I did not even believe in myself and for helping me realize my dream of getting my first book into production.

Thank you to my parents who gave me a second chance when no one else would, in this case water is thicker than blood. Big thank you to my best friend who has always been there and has made me go on even when I wanted to lay down and give up. Thanks Mary Byassee Jones, my favorite partner in crime!

In closing I would like to thank life for giving me many heartaches, happiness and so many other reasons to write the words that fall from my heart.

Bathsheba Dailey - fairytailbaby@gmail.com

Edited, Formatted, and Cover Art by True Beginnings Publishing.. All Illustrations, Cover Art, and text is Copyright Protected by My Original Works. Reference # 52364.

First Printing, 2013
ISBN-13: 978-0615887050
ISBN-10: 0615887058

Ordering Information:
Quantity sales. Special discounts are available on quantity purchases by corporations, associations, and others. For details, contact the Author at the address above.

To order additional copies of this book, please visit:
https://www.createspace.com/4441643

Hearts and Souls Poetry Book © made possible by and through. Photography book cover provided by Patt Martin. Interior Photography of Train Tracks/Girl and Boy Walking provided by Moyer Photos September 18, 2009 using a Nikon D200 under Attribution Creative Common License.

Table of Contents

Bathsheba Dailey

Tracks of Life

Lost on the tracks of life,
never to know should I turn left or a right.

Speeding by me like a train without a destination,
my life is fueled by hesitation.

Loudness to be heard all around me,
a thousand words my mind is always telling me.

Pebbles of the unseen to stay under my feet,
scared of where these tracks may lead me.

A bridge that needs to be crossed!

Wishing life would for once be clear,
I am tired of always feeling lost and in fear.

Lost on the tracks of life,
walking down this road that seems so rough.

Wondering did I take the right turn,
these tracks under my feet I burn.

Looking from the way that I just came,
should I of continued from that way?

It is too late to turn back now,
these are the tracks of life that I am bound.

Always Love

In and out of my life you have been,
at one time we were merely just friends.

Thrown together by the chance of fate,
a friendship that grew stronger every day.

Years went by so very fast,
the time came when I had to find now my own path.

Never to realize what I gave up,
just a very young girl wanting to make it on her own.

Years now to go slowly by,
never forgetting the first love of my life.

In my life he came again,
now our love grew stronger than it had ever been.

Stories of our lives to be shared at first,
then dreams of what was ahead for us.

Out again this time by him,
now my heart will never really love again.

Dreams of him in and out of my mind,
my days now full of what should of been.

Bathsheba Dailey

Soul Mates for Life

No words could ever define
the way you broke this heart of mine,
tears never to stop leaving my eyes.
A heart that is forever entwined.

My days go by slowly dying
like a rose on an severed vine.
The pedals lightly hitting the ground,
not a living one is to be found.

Leaves turning browner every day,
no longer do I feel like I am flying high
singing a song as the wind blows by.
Like a songbird who lost his wing,
never again to hear him sing.

Like a killer whale under the sea,
losing the one that was meant to be.
Never again to find another mate,
they only love the one that was brought by fate.

Never again will my mind and heart be set free,
all these things is how I felt when you left me.
Blinded by the light when I wake up at dawn,
already knowing the new tears that shall fall.

Poisoned Veins

I will meet you in the Heavens above to fulfill our dreams,
the ones we wished for here,
but the world denied us of.

Battles to be lost to those who could never understand,
that you have and always will be my lover and best friend.

Our hearts cannot be denied,

when we leave this world we will never again have to hide
what we have always felt inside.

Two people with a different outlook on life,

two people that in so many ways are the perfect pair, no
one else compares.

We never again will have to hide our smiles, never again
have to hear we will never be... no one has walked our
miles to be.

No more lies will we believe because when we meet on the other side we will see the lies told in deceit.

You say if it does not happen here then you know it will when we go away,
so if this is true fill my veins with poison so I can be with you only.

Swift Kisses

Love softly blow me a kiss,
in your arms I am never to be dismissed.

My body is taken over by your sweet love and passion,
when I am with you there is nothing more for the asking.

A tremble in my legs as you hold me up,
an earthshaking movement as we make love.
Leave me again with promises of tomorrow,

chase away my nightmares of horror.
Tell me I am beautiful as I am,
a better woman cannot be found.

Give me your heart and soul,
my love for you will never grow old.
A poem to reach you by far, memories that I cannot part.

A swift kiss to my cheek,
as you come up behind and hold me.

A love to never be beat,
a love so true you found in me. Love to never be out done;
I will still be missing you when the morning comes.

Deep breaths
Holding on to all of our memories,
listening still to the words you would have me to always
believe.

I have proven time and time again that I would do anything
to make you be proud to be my man.
But sitting here alone I still am,
just the same as when we first began.

Wondering why life has to be so cruel,
using my heart against me like a sharpened tool.
My mind believed all that it was told,
my body now has grown so cold.

My heart now I shall scold,
for believing that I finally had a love to hold.
Taking again a deep breath, wishing it would be my last.

Unspoken Words

My mind weighs heavily with unspoken words,
like bricks that hold you down never to turn loose of your
body.

So many words spoken with no meaning,
just wanting for once to hear something that is said with
feelings and wanting.

The devil knocks on your door with so many stories
never to hear explanations leaves me with an endless
worry.

Putting a smile on my face can only go on for so long,
always wondering what I am to him,
leaves me with a longing.

Never to understand the feelings I hold for him,
just waiting for the words that are always to come,
in my heart you are the one,
in my mind I cannot yet move on.

Torn to pieces, crumbled like dry leaves,
all I have ever asked for is a reason to truly believe
that this is more than a mere dream.

Tears to always leave my eyes,
with the words I am always made to disguise.

A knot in my throat,
feeling like there is no more hope.

Told to be happy with what I have,
never to think that I just want what the other one has
always had, nothing more but a fighting chance.

I will go along my day as I always do;
only thinking of you.
Knowing she has so much more because you
are too scared to cut the strings completely through.

My eyes will cry another tear, as my heart beats in misery,
never to understand the words he is never to speak.

The Dreams We Shared

Our dreams we shall always share,

like the sky shares itself with the stars above and the
hillside will always share itself with the beauty
of the wildflowers that coats the flushing green grass that
grows beneath it.

The nights we shared will always be here in the depth of my
heart that I bare.
I will always remember how it felt to be in your arms and I
still feel a shiver
when thinking of your breath softly tickling my neck.

I can still hear you softly singing in my ear,

our bodies and hearts could not of been any closer as you
played lightly in my hair
and we slow danced showing the love that we have always
shared.

When I sleep I dream of the sweet smile on your face as
your eyes glistened with what could of only been stars
pulled straight from
the sparkling sky and placed in your beautiful eyes.

The dreams we shared will always be here, I am just waiting
for you my dear.
My soul waits for the only man who carries her mate and
my heart shall not ever fall for another,
I shall always wait for my soul mate.

Hearts to Break

She always does as he wishes,
even knowing he is fake
only wanting to find another way to break
the one he has for so long told to wait.

He dismisses all he has done,
not ever caring of the harm that has went on.
Her heart had not ever mattered,
he leaves her torn and tattered.

She remembers so much of lives past,
wishes so badly she had not made such changes.
Wishing she had seen sooner,
he was the one who would in the end destroy her.

Telling her she is better off than the one whom enjoyed to
see her bleed,
never to realize her heart was still alive but now dead as the
fall leaves.

He dared to say she was the one he had waited for,
knowing in his heart she had only been one of his little
whores.

A year wasted thinking he loved her.
Another wasted as his little dummy,
as always he said he loved me. Wait and suffer,
my life being nothing more than his little Muppet.

Hearts and Souls

A little lie to him destroying more of what she had been.
A drunk she is,
no care of even the littlest things.

A happy girl she had once been.
Even with her arms broke and eyes so black,
but at least her heart was intact.

He cares not of what he has put her through,
he only thinks his life should be true,
never really caring about me or you.

He wishes for so much in life,
he cares not of what he so easily can destroy.

A look from his baby blues,
tearing hearts into two!
A sweet word to be said,
anything to get you into bed!

A heart to be broke forever,
thinking he was the one who would take her to heaven.

The cold goes through her skin, thinking of so much of his
hurtful games. To believe he ever cared is silly,
a stupid girl was me. He thinks he done right,
he believes he deserves more,
but why if just his silly little whore.

One, two and three how many more can there be?
Just silly girls thinking of only he.

A heart he can break,
and then laugh at their mistakes.

Only he will ever know,
why he thinks that their hearts are not ones to care for in
his little show.

Vowed Words

I am a better person than I have perceived to be,
for just a moment losing all of my sanity.
A heart torn only to be scorned,
for loving the one person who it adored.

No more can take me down.

From here on out I will no longer feel any doubt,
I know in my heart what we had.
No one can tare that apart,

no one can make me believe in anything else
but what he said and breathed.
Hearts to linger on together, no matter where we are,
it has been like this forever.

I will love him no matter where we are at,
and in his mind I know he will always hear the words I
vowed.
Loving him until the end of our days, our true feelings never
to go away.
I do not believe any longer I was played, I hear of this every
day.

Too scared to be together,
too scared to be apart
but knowing one day our love will find its way.

No matter how far apart we may be,
together our hearts has always known
the true meaning of love and best friends,
there is no use to try and pretend
that together we have always been meant.

I will wait as I always have,

I will remember the words he has handed,
to love me more than any other man.
A true love to be stuck in turmoil,
a true love to be soiled!
Stuck in the middle of all that will never be understood, I
was lead to him by the glittering stars and moon.
A dream of him as I fall asleep,
in my heart he shall always be.

Unfolded

Some to never understand, others to never forget.
Some to go on blindly through their days, others cannot
remember anything else but those days.

Some to go on in the life that is set out to play,
others not wanting to live
long enough to feel yet more vengeful pain.

Hearts to never know the boundaries they could of shared,
too scared to see what was always hidden there.

Minds to play tricks of a life worth forgetting!
Twinkling stars in the sky,
the beauty you had always wished to find.

A place better than here,
a place to dream of without any tears.

Seasons Change

Soft petals on the rose bushes to die away the trees turning
so many different shades.
A cool breeze whistling outside reminding us of the seasons
change.

A dew settles overnight making the grass seem a beautiful
covered shade of white.
Anticipation for winter to come,
the snowflakes falling in so many shapes.

Whiteness covering the hills and branches of what was so
green, a beauty so surreal and free.

Waiting for the first spring flower to arrive!
Waking up to such a surprise, a beauty that was hiding.

Seasons change as this world spins on, a new season to be
born.
A new beauty to adore!

Painful Memories

Sitting there listening to songs of heartache, so badly
wanting so much more,
but to always be living in the past being reminded of
tormented mistakes.

Living in fear to be truly loved,
worrying once again that your mind and heart will be hurt
and never to be understood.

A man to sit alone in a full room,
wanting to be found in such a world full of gloom.
As perfect as he is,
he still thinks he deserves nothing more than the pain he
always feels knocking at his door.

Always to put his dreams on hold,
never to realize one day he too will grow old. Never to give
himself the love he deserves,
always feeling like his heart and life should stay on reserve,
to always worry about everyone else as his life sits on a
shelf.

Another bottle to be opened up,
another song of long ago to be played,
his heart in so much misery.
Too scared to take the first step,
so worried his life once again will be one to forget.

One and the same they seem to be,
both feeling like life set out to give them nothing more than
miseries.
A life to be found with a true love,
the one who will understand the feelings that haunts each
other's hearts.

The dreams that for so long have been set in the dark, their
hearts never to part.

Happy Memories

So long I have sat in the dark remembering
everything we were and all that we shared.
So badly wanting back the one
who always had that tender word that could always make
my heart flutter,
and wishing for so much more.

Sitting with the one who has always made me a better
person, loving everything about him,
not wanting him to change in anyway.
For the first time in forever I can smile,
a real smile not made up of lies.
No more disguise,
my heart to flutter again as I look into his beautiful eyes.

Something to play on my mind though,
torturing the happiness I can only find with him,
am I really the one he wishing to find.
A terror touches my heart as my soul once again feels torn
apart,
a tear is to leave my eyes in a hopelessness my life always
seems to find.

Bathsheba Dailey

My love truer than it has ever been,
my heart wanting the one who has always been my best
friend.

How can I tell what is true or not,
when my mind is closed off to my heart's desire.

I sit and wonder so many things, my heart to cry a million
tears,
hoping this is the beginning of many happy memories.

A Love Written in the Stars

Tender touches reminding me of happier days.
Kisses being lightly left on my body
leaving me to shudder
with the passion that is being bestowed upon me.

His body pressed against mine,
legs to shake as they always do when in his arms.
Pleasures to be found in the sweet love I so crave,
never will I want to leave this place.

A kiss to his face, feeling him close to me.
Knowing in each other's arms we have always meant to be.
This love was written in the stars that I have prayed on for
so long. He is in my heart and his heart is where I want to
always belong.

Happy graceful steps when I leave this place, hoping to have
many more of these splendid days.

Loving him has always been what has set my heart and soul
to rest, he has always brought out in me my best.

Another kiss to his cheek I shall leave,
my mind to of finally found release.
Reminding myself that it is truly he that holds me.

Life's Gift

My life has fallen into place,
loving arms and words to take away the tears that for so
long fell from my face.

A life of dreams to chase,
feeling so right when with the one they were made.
Eyes to shine with the love of my life,
loving him more tonight.

My spirits has been uplifted,
I feel like my life has now finally been given the best gift of
all.
A man who I knew would catch me before I fall.

Always to be at my best when I am with him,
my heart could never of dreamt for a better man.
One that I can trust,
one to give everything I am.

In his arms I feel the safest,
a love I could never replace.
Souls to match and hearts to speak,
the life I always dreamed....

Hearts and Souls

Shade of Blue

It is true this heart I beat has always been for you,
it has turned a shade of blue as it beats to a new tune.

My heartbeat weakens as it has to endure another day
without you,
taking breathless beats just enough to get me through to a
new day
that I would rather share with you.

As each day passes a new heartbreak shall come,
every day without you here makes me go a little bit more
numb.

My heart cries out to yours,
I still feel that our love is true.
I will never give up in believing that it should of always been
me and you.

Too much has been said and too much has been done,
but in the end a heart can lie none.

Bathsheba Dailey

Be Stilled Heart

He be stills my heart with the tenderness he speaks,
the dreams that he has and all of his memories.

He has a spell on my heart one that seems to always be
there,
no matter not how much I may feel and hurt.

His soul beckons for mine to wake,
to drift away from our bodies in an attempt to escape our
lives.

My mind speaks loving words to him that needs not be
spoken,
for I know they will find their way to him.

My pulse races when I sleep of a night dreaming of
him until the day breaks and I shall be relieved only when I
wake.

My Girls

They give me peace of mind even as they try to wear me
down.
They can make me smile when I thought none could be
found.

They show me why I am here and what life should really be
about.
Even when they get mad at me and sit around and pout.

They can make me madder than I have ever been
but with one smile and kiss I am turned to mush, again.

I love them more than they will ever know,
they are my life and always will be my three baby girls,
no matter what age.

Emptiness

My mind is a blank but yet so full of thoughts that seem to
never go away.
You have moments in your life when all seems right and
your mind has no time to stray.
My heart is empty but yet it is full of life and reasons to
continue on.
My soul sleeps for now waiting on what it needs to once
again breath and wander while I rest of a night,
my soul is waiting to feel again and make another flight.

My heart beats at a slow pace waiting for that unknown
someone to make it race once again.
I am confused again as it seems I have always been,
I just want to look into someone's eyes and see what has
been missing.

Professed Love

He comes toward her professing his love to her as he had
done many times before,
but this time she feels her heart is unsure.

She grazes her hand gently down his cheek,

as she says this time I will not let you break me.

She slowly turns to walk away from him as he grabs her arm
and says please believe me for I had never meant to deceive
thee.

The tears start to trickle from her eyes as she says unto him
I will not fall anymore for your lies.

She gazes upon his face one last time as she flees from him
and all of his lies.

All That I Shall Ask of Thee

All that I shall ask of thee is to be true and loving only to
me.
I ponder in the stillness of night wondering what shall
become of our lives.

I shudder at each step you take coming toward me as I
slowly wake.
I can feel my heart pitter patter
as you lay your hand lovingly against my body.

My legs start to tremble and my hands begin to shake, this
is what I have been dreaming of,
to feel your breath softly against my neck and to taste the
lust that comes from your sweet lips.

All I shall ask of thee is to be true and loving only to me.
Make no mistake in the light of dawn for I cannot take any
more heartache
as I listen to another meaningless song.

I open my eyes as you fade away leaving through the
window in which you had come.
I race to the window and move the curtains aside and yell
out to you in one more heart wrenching cry,
all that I ask of thee is to be true and loving only to me.

Nature's Greatness

A rose petal opens to perfection,
as a bird sings in beautiful harmony.

A fawn is playfully strutting along as his mother calls for him
to follow.
A breeze is swiftly blowing your hair,
as you can hear the leaves softly flowing.

A baby is born and you can hear her first cry,
as she looks for the first time into her mother's loving eyes.

A rainbow is left behind after the thrusting of rain, leaving
the air with the smell of being freshly cleaned.

You can hear the waters rushing to shore from the ocean,
as you lean back in the sand you think to yourself how can
you ask for anything more!

A True Father

It's been twenty years and we have shared many memories, tears, laughs and everything that says you are my one true Dad.

I was a lost soul who was said could never be saved but I found my smile in such a saving grace.

We have went through many things but to ever leave was something I could never do, my heart as your daughter is one that rang true.

You helped me build my self-esteem even when I couldn't see why you always believed in me.

The memory's we have shared is ones that I will have with no other because you are my one true father.

Hearts and Souls

A New Day

It seems like my heart has been ripped from my chest,
no matter how much I tried, I just wasn't enough.

I can feel my blood running through your fingers as you look
at it and throw it to the ground,
leaving me with nothing but a lingering heartless frown.

My life was really nothing that special
but it was one that left me with more than a nervous
tremble.

You told me there was so much more in this world to see
you were the one who wanted to guild me.

I went to bed every night with a smile on my face
and there was no mistaking the light I felt in your grace.

I waited for you as you told me to do,
waiting for all of our dreams to come true.
I wondered how much longer I would have to wait

and how many more steps you would ask me to take.
I waited for you as you told me what to do
my heart was one that was faithful and true.

Bathsheba Dailey

I cannot think of anymore
I could of done to prove to you that I was the one.

You told me you could never let me go,
we were so much alike we would never feel alone.
You said this felt so right and asked me to not give up this
fight.

You said in the end we would be together no matter what
storms we would have to weather,
us being as one was all that had mattered.

I sit here alone now and I cannot help but look at my phone
wishing it would ring with that voice on the other end that
could always make my heart sing.

As I lay my head down on my pillow
I cry so many tears of heart wrenching sorrow.
My life is nothing now that have have gone away it seems
so hard to wake up to the light of day.

As the dawn breaks unto a new day
I cannot help but wonder what it will bring.
As the moon sets in the big black sky
I know once again I will go to bed with tear drops falling
from my eyes.

Heartbeats

The air that I breath is filled with your sweet scent,
it seems as though my body is completely spent.

The heartbeats I take are ones filled with so many mistakes,
and the thoughts on my mind are ones that are not so
divine.

The trust that I laid right in your hands was something I
knew
I could never chance,
but this I done at your command.

My soul cries out for its second half,
and in you that's what I thought I had finally found.
My blood rushes and boils under my skin,
I can't help but wonder how I could of ever let you in.

The tears that I cry are ones made from all of your lies,
but even in knowing this I could never hate you or even
despise.

For you I could never wish anything but the best, and for
me I wish nothing more than a peaceful rest.
In my heart you will always be,
this is something I know will always be true, my mind still
wonders if it is the same for you.

Bathsheba Dailey

Best Friends and Lovers

The blossoms on the tress has withered away, the fog
seems to of blacken the sky, through the light of day.

I try to listen to the songbird sing,

but its sweet voice is one that I will never hear again.

I look up at the stars that once shone so bright,

but now I feel as if I am being swallowed into the night.

I close my eyes to disappear from the world, yet even there
my dreams are ones of turmoil.

I look into the future to see what may be, but all I can see is
a girl that once was me.

I drop to my knees and pray to feel again, there is no use
because I have lost my true love and the best friend that I
had found in you.

He Can No Longer Run

The tears we have cried,
the nights families have dreaded of knowing there loved
one will never come back from the dead!!

The years have flown by and some had even wondered if
their daughter, father, mother and very dear sons murderer
would ever come to justice.

So many troops have gave their all
spending many nights crying for their families that they left
behind.

We count the loss of so many that have died in search of
the man that they could never
find bringing tears to all Americans eyes.

This is a day we can all be proud of even our loved ones
that still lays buried in the twin towers ground,
our fallen troops that is so far away and may never be
found.

Even with the loudness of all our cheers
we can never forget the fallen tears that has soaked the
pillows of Americans for so many years.

So let us all cheer and give high fives because the time has
come
where Bin Laden can no longer run and hide!

Let us not forget the troops that are still so far away,
for they have taken a stand to protect you and me,
no matter the cost to them and their families.

Special Indeed

You look at me and what do you see?
I am special yes I am indeed.....

As you see me being wheeled on by,
I can sometimes feel the tears you want to cry!

You think me weak and feel sorry for me,
but I am stronger than most will ever be!

I see this world with different eyes,
ones that cannot see hate or despise.

So when you see me being wheeled on by
look at my smile I never hide...

So yes I am special indeed,
and I will never want to be anyone else but me.

Always

On my mind you will always be,
day and night and always in my dreams.

In my heart you will always be and the miles that separate
us makes no difference to me.

I feel you day and night
you are always on my mind even in my sleep.

A part of my soul belongs to you!
We are not two but one, can you feel this too my love?

You are my true love this I am sure of.
I have never felt this before and I never will again.

We are one and the same,
we can feel each other's haunting pain.

We read each other's minds,
we know what the other is thinking all the time,
buried in each other's mind.

When we fight I feel like you will drive me insane yet to lose
your love would be the worse pain.

Hearts and Souls

I wonder when we will be together
I pray when that day comes we will be forever.

I love you with all of my heart, body, mind and soul
I cannot wait until the day you are mine.

Until then know this to be true,
I will always be here waiting for you.

Bathsheba Dailey

Thunderstorm

The rolling of the thunder that lays just beneath the
heavens sky,
a flash of lightning that you can just see glimmer
out of the corner of your eye.

The hill crest cannot be seen for the fog and blackened
trees. You can still hear the rumble of the storm as it passes
you by,
leaving nothing behind except for the wetness that fell from
the sky.

It leaves you with a peace of mind knowing it did not have
to be so kind, it could have left nothing behind the roaring
thunder and down pouring skies!

The smell in the air is so refreshing and you cannot wait to
see the spring flowers this will bring,
and in the distance you can hear the wildlife as it sings.
As you hear the last of the thunder rumbling underneath
the sky,
you are amazed to see lightning once again flashing
but this time it is saying goodbye!

Hearts and Souls

Holder of My Heart

You hold my heart in the palm of your hand,
I feel it pulse more and more the closer you are.

I have never known a greater man one who makes me feel
more special than I really am.
The day can be long and the sky can be gray but to hear
your voice always makes my day.

There can be a thousand clouds in the sky
but none of them can overcast the beautiful smile on your
face and the twinkle that is always in your eyes.
You hold my heart in the palm of your hand
I hope you know to me you are the greatest man.

Day and night, awake and asleep
I believe that we are really meant to be.

You hold my heart in the palm of your hand and I am so
happy to know that you are my man. My body cries for your
touch,
your arms around me means so much
to feel your lip's on my face there could be no other to take
your place.

When your day is long and the sky is full of gray just
remember...
***

I am only a heartbeat away.

Just in Case You May Wonder

Just in case you may wonder
I think of you every day
you make me laugh with the things you say.

Just in case you may wonder
my heart melts when you look at me that way.

Just in case you may wonder
you put a smile on my face with just thinking of your tight
embrace.

Just in case you may wonder
you are the only one I dream of in my slumber.

My Love

My love for you will never go astray
even when you seem so far away....

The air I breathe has your sweet scent,
this love I feel is heaven sent.

As the days grow longer the nights move so slow
my love for you has only grown.

In my dreams I see your sweet face
it takes me to the most wonderful place.

I think of you all the time
I wonder if you will ever be mine.

My love for you will never go astray
in my dreams I am with you every day.

Bathsheba Dailey

The Ocean

The sand is soft under my feet
I can feel the water as it rushes to me.

The tide is coming in
I can smell the salt in the wind.

I rush out to the ocean,
I want to feel the water all over me one more time.

The water is so deep and so are my thoughts
I feel a freedom and it's all I have got.

I can feel the tide rushing in faster but I still do not want to
get out because that is not what I am after.

I love to feel the sand rolling over my feet
the salt in the air that I am breathing is so sweet.

In the water is where I feel the safest it's the most beautiful
place.
I take a deep breath, I know it is time to go ashore

I want to feel the water over me just once more, before I go
ashore.

Always Miss You Some

The years flew by so very fast,
now I am to live in the past.

So many hard times I can still remember today,
but I also remember also the happy memories.

I remember the days when nothing ever could break
our gaze nothing could ever make me go away.

I cry when I think of those times,
not to remember your heartbreaking lies.

What I miss the most is having someone to hold me,
someone who seemed to need me.

The days are getting easier as they go one by one on by,
but to say I do not miss you some would only be a lie.

Mindset

My mind is reeling over and over,
my heart is beating out of control.

I no deep down it's done and over
but in my heart I cannot let go.

What do you do when you feel this way?
When it is all you think about every day.

My mind is telling me to make a new start,
but deep down inside I feel as though we could never be
apart.

What do you do when you feel this way?
when it is all you think about every day.

I am so tired I just wish I could sleep,
I wish my heart would slow its beat.

I wish my mind would let me be,
let me see what needs to be.

So what do you do when you feel this way?
when it's all you think about every day.

Sunset

The sun has set the moon is out,
beautiful stars are shinning all about.

There is a cool breeze just slightly so,
just enough to make your hair lightly blow.

The air is so sweet
it makes my heart want to skip a beat.

In the night comes a peacefulness
that makes my heart want to explode with bliss.

In this place I would like to stay
and feel this freedom and joy every day.

Bathsheba Dailey

No More Wasted Tears

The cold I feel in my heart is for the wasted time
I know we should of been apart.

I tried my best but I failed the test,
I cannot help but think of all the rest.

All the years I wasted in tears,
all the day's I wasted in a daze.
Why did it have to come to this?
What in the world did I miss?

I never thought this would be us,
never thought that I would catch that bus,
the one leading me away from you and trying to start my
life anew.

It is going to be hard there's no doubt about that,
but this is one test I won't fail at.

The time has come the day is here
where I refuse to waste another tear on you my dear.

Fear and Pain

Bring me fear, bring me pain,
bring me anything that will make me feel again.

Give me your heart... tell me your dreams
let me see your soul and all that it feels.

If you needed me yesterday then need me today,
my love is not one that will ever stray.

Be my friend today and be my friend tomorrow
let our friendship not be one of sorrow.

My friendship is not one you can pick and choose
to want only when you are feeling

Blue because there are times when
I need you too!

Give me your heart,
give me your soul our love is one yet to be unfolded.

Tell me your wishes... tell me your dreams,
I will do anything that you need.

Bring me fear; bring me pain.
All I want is to feel again!

First Steps

You breath your life into a child the moment that they are
conceived, waiting for the day you two shall meet.

You hold them tight in your arms
and in your heart from then on they shall always be,
loving every moment happily.

You listen to them as they cackle and coo waiting for the
day you hear them call for you.

You watch them as they take their first step,
so scared that they may trip.

Holding your arms as wide as can be,
motioning them to walk toward you slowly.

You watch them as they grow wondering where the time
has gone,
remembering all the stories and lullabies songs.

Your babies grow up and move on into this big old world
where there is so much turmoil.

You cannot help but want to keep them small
protecting them from everything and all.

A Parents Love and Loss

How divine to look down at such a sweet face,
cherishing every minute we shared in this place.
We watched as you fought your battle so strong,
at times it seemed as if you could not be so small.

We watched your eyelids as they moved in your sleep
a tiny smile that seemed to glow on your face so sweetly.
We now wonder if you already knew what was getting
ready to take place.
Did you know you were going to live with our heavenly
father at such a young age?

We feel such sorrow for the loss that we have had to bare,
but we will always remember the love and smiles that were
shared.
To feel you in our arms once more

is something that we will have to wait for,
when we come home to you with our heavenly father
we can then be together forever more.

Until we meet again you will always be in our hearts and
souls,
loving you was the best test of all.

Bathsheba Dailey

Walk With Me

Walk with me down this path I shall take,
walking it by myself is a long and dark road.

Don't walk behind me for I am no better than you,
don't walk in front of me because you are no better than I.

Walk beside me hand in hand seeing the world for all it has
to offer us,
together we shall walk down this new path.

Look at me as you speak my name
seeing me for the person I am
as I will look at you the same as I speak your name.

When you hold me don't hold me light press my body to
yours in a tight embrace as I will hold yours just the same.

Walk with me down this path that we shall take,
our lives is one that only we can change.

Together we can make a difference,
hand in hand we shall be loving each other and all the we
can be.

Maybe One Day

Leave me not to feel despair,
beg me not to go away but give me your life that needs me
so, even though your mind sees it not,
our hearts cannot be apart.

Your treading on a path that will not bring you the true
happiness you so desire
always worried about the outcome that you yet cannot see.

You give yourself to what everyone else wants
never realizing they care not of your own heart
and of what it truly needs to make your life something
other than an hopeless dream.

You live your life for other people never doing what you
wish for the most,
always punishing yourself for the wrong you think you have
done not realizing
even you deserve true love and a happiness
you cannot find with anyone else but "the one."

You fight a battle within yourself making your life one of
your own made hell.
You deny yourself of all happiness
no matter what the cost may be to you.

You know I speak the truth in all that I say
so I have only one question for you so please answer me.
When will your own life be one that you try to please?

I guess this we will have to see, I guess maybe
you will one day live for yourself and all of your dreams.

Bathsheba Dailey

Love Song

Run your hand slightly up my back,
giving me the slightest shiver as you reach my nape.

Bring your mouth slowly to mine
just teasing me with the breath that I can barely feel.

Pull me up to your body holding me tightly,
looking deep into my eyes in a searching gaze.

Dance with me slowly never moving at all
just our bodies dancing in an endless song.

Let our hearts beat together as we lose our breath
just to feel each other seems to be enough.

Shower your love down on me,
never doing more than letting our bodies sing this romantic
love song together.

Hearts and Souls

Lingering Memories

Footsteps left imprinted on my heart,
of my true love that I never thought I would be apart.
Teardrops from a soul that can find no other
like the one she shared with her other half and true lover.
Traces of memories lingering on my mind
of a love lost that no one could ever define.

Two bodies that roamed as they pleased
never knowing the words of they can't or boundaries.
Dreams of all they were going to do
never giving a thought that their lives were coming to an
end as two.

A heart that will never beat it's hardest again
as her soul cries for what could have been.
Precious memories put on a shelf
as her body lays down
dreaming of a life that she shall share with no one else.

Bathsheba Dailey

Fallen Leaves

I love the fall and all that it brings,
feeling on my face it's gentle breeze.
Walking in the forest inclined to my own thoughts.

Hearing the leaves crackle under my feet,
out of the corner of my eye,
catching a glimpse of a deer
as it jumps across a fallen tree.

Hearing the birds as they sing a beautiful song,
seeing all the colors the trees
have become proving once more it is fall..

Sleeping Smiles

Laying there looking so sweet,
hair falling in your face as you sleep
dreaming of childhood things.
Seeing your lips as they curl in a smile
bringing a smile of my own.

Hearing a whimper as you sleep,
making me worry of what you see in your dream.
Pushing your hair back as I kiss your little cheek telling you
everything is okay, it was just a dream,
watching you drift back to sleep.

Regretting any argument we may of had that day
as I watch your sweetness as you sleep.
Wanting to keep you young,
I never want you to be out on your own.

I may be being selfish
but to ever see you get hurt just kills me.
I watch you as you sleep and hold you closely to me,
in hopes you will never leave me.
A smile once again touches your face
as I give you another loving embrace.

Bathsheba Dailey

Sweet Memories

A breathless whisper of love in my ear
makes my heart and soul shed a tear,
of sweet nights I remember so clearly.
Holding me tightly in your embrace,
chasing all of my fears away.
I fall asleep with those sweet memories
of the one who means the world to me....

Hidden Pain

When will my life ever be more than just a world,
I have to exist in?

How can I make my family and friends happy,
when I am not happy myself?

What brings me down to this level at any given time?
Why do I cry these tears, of extreme pain?

Where is my life leading me?
Who can answer these questions that I ask?

Bathsheba Dailey

The Right Timing

Treacherous hearts looking for ones to break!
How many tears can one human cry?
When do the games of fun come to an end?

How many sleepless nights will it take?
To fall asleep not thinking of you a bit!
How many times will I cry out for you?
How many times will you ignore this to?

When do I make the first move out?
Not just one that I regret in the end!
How many times will I beg forgiveness?
Drawing you to our secret meeting place!

When will I know the time is right?
When will I give up on this hopeless fight?
How many times will I hear the same story?
How many times will you tell it?

Time is running out for you and me!
When will you let fate take its place?
How many times can I drift off to sleep,
tears drying on my reddened cheeks?

How will I know when the time is right?
If you are too scared to fight the fight!
Are we to just let things be as they are?
When we die who will regret the most?

I have fought the fight,
now it's your turn to make it right!

All That We Can Be

Why do we question ourselves?
We can only be as good as we can be,
loving the ones who show they really care.

Why do we feel as if we need to be more
When our friends show us we are great
just the way we are!

Why do we fight a battle that needs not to be won?
When we know we have done all that we could!
The rest is something that has to be just be understood.

When do we see what others see in us?
A disappointment is all that we see in ourselves,
a life that seems to not be enough!

When do we stand up and love ourselves?
Knowing we have done our best,

and the rest is left to the ones we love the most.
In hopes that our friends and family can just understand!

Relentless Words

Words seem to always be on my mind,
a relentless hold on me until it is released into a perfect
rhyme or something else to my divine...

thoughts racing through my head never to let me rest!
My dreams are overtaken by the things I wish to write,
for some reason not coming together when I turn on my
light.

A frustration takes me away,

What were the words I wanted to say?
Hours on end wanting to shut off my thoughts,
swirling around my head,
won't my mind ever stop?
Thoughts racing around my mind,
what shall I write about this time?
Thoughts as always never to stop,
it is once again time to grab a pen and start to jot.

Hidden Feelings

I hold my head down! Not in embarrassment,
but not wanting you to see what my eyes will show you,
hiding from it is the best for both!

I act as if you are not everything to me,
not wanting you to see you are the only person for me.

I hold a giggle in,
scared that I laugh at everything you say.
Giving away that, I hold every word to my heart..
I am just to scared to tell you afraid you should part.

I give you private glances,
turning away when your eyes look toward me.
Scared to death you had just caught me.
I feel your eyes on me,

I wonder do you like what you see and then it crosses me,
how could I of been so unaware?
That it is just not me scared to share my feelings.

Who goes first me or you?
Should we keep hiding?
Or should we see where this will go?
Do we live to regret the one we may unwilling let go?

Bathsheba Dailey

The Wait

Why do I waste my time?
Talking to you can make me lose my mind!
You leave me with tears in my eyes!
I am sure to you this leaves you with no surprise.

Why do I pour my heart out... to you?
Why do you always say we are true?
Why do you leave me this way?
Am I just a heart to be played?

Why do I waste my time with you?
Don't you realize this is not what a heart conceives to be
true?
What makes me stay?
With you my mind always strays.

When will this heartache go away?
When will you mutter the words?
That brings me joy?

How much more can I take?
How much more of my heart can you break?
When will you see,
that I am all that you say you need?
What makes you shy away?
Why do we have to wait for another day?
What is it you need from me...to stay?

Hearts and Souls

How can you say I am all and more that you need?
When you are not here with me!
How much longer can we wait?
How much longer will we test fate?

Our lives are not ones to be counted on,
one day one will leave the other,
just for you to regret what was never...

Games We Play

Drift to sleep thinking about you,
in my dreams you could be nothing other than true to me.

Nightmares haunt my days, most the time I sit in a gaze.
God the games that were played!

A song lingers in the back ground,
my mind goes to our last dance.
I remember every move we made,
as the song softly played.

Your lips touching my neck so tenderly,
how I wish my true love was still here with me!

I settle down in hopes to rest,
but my mind won't let me be so blessed.

Thinking of you is all have left,
I wish you would walk back through my door.

My heart would explode loving you
...forever more....

Sitting in a Corner

Sitting in a corner, trapped no way out...
fights a battle within herself,
all to lose... nothing to win.

Forces keeping her slumped over in that corner!
Not wanting to make the wrong move,
not knowing what the right one is...

Fighting a battle within herself,
tears fall not knowing which way to go.
To keep on the track she is on has killed all her beliefs.

To give up now may be the biggest mistake.

Sits in a corner, trapped no way out...
Looking to the future,
or to keep living in the past!

Bathsheba Dailey

Time to Heal

My love cannot be found here anymore,
my many tears flooding the bedroom floor...

Remembering our nights in this room,
a man I thought would never leave me...

My heart is breaking as I think of your name,
I only could wish you felt the same...

My body shakes as I remove your things,
from my life and now my daydreams...

A love like that takes time to heal,
but in my arms I wish you were where I could always feel...

I know it is time to move on,
but how hard it is when I hear our song...

My arms feel empty now that you are away,
a love like that takes time to fade away...

I dream of you when I lay my head down to sleep,
my dreams making me wake up to weep...

I think of you every day,
wishing you would come back to me...

Never to be Forgotten

They sat high above the ground,
so true and fearlessly proud.
So tall they could almost reach the beautiful clouds,
to be seen for the first time would leave you in awe.

A city so strong and proud,
coming to its knees as they were left to beg pleading for
mercy and peace.

Running in all directions not knowing where to go, scared of
what may happen next and was this really it.
Wondering if their families were safe from harm,
or were they facing this tragedy afar.

The blue skies are now flaming with fire,
all around in disbelief and despair.
Even building made so strong,
could not with hold this heat.
Even they had been defeated.

Men and woman alike risk their lives
as they do every day and night.
This battle was one they could not fight.
A city destroyed in a matter of moments,
People's hopes and dreams ruined as they fall to the
ground.

Another plane crashes into the towers,
now all hope of getting to safety are devoured.
Smoke and fire fill the city, lungs to be left to suffocate.
The brutal smoke cannot be escaped.

Bathsheba Dailey

Towers now falling to the ground,
pieces of once great buildings are soon not to be found.
What had started as a beautiful morning,
was now nothing more than dust to be found on a deadly
blackened ground.

Firefighters are tormented by all the lives they could not
save, the twin towers now nothing more than burning
graves.
Rubble to be looked at by all,
cheered on by the men who had made our twin towers fall.

A city left with no more hope as they run away from endless
explosions.
A sad story was to be told by the eyes of all that now lay
cold.
A city once held so strong
now cries for their families and loved ones that are gone.
Always in their hearts never to be forgotten....

Waiting for the Unknown

At this point there is not anything holding me here in this place of dread and heartache any longer. I sit here and wait for the unknown to happen day in and day out. I hear the same words being spoken as I have heard for so long now. I let myself be hurt over and over being told that I am special and the choice was one that was not wanted, but yet here I sit in a darkened room waiting for the unknown as I have done for so long now.

I play our songs and remember all the stories and dreams we could trust with no one else over in my head every day. I am told the battle is not over yet that one day things will be as it should of been, but yet I sit here waiting for the unknown, all alone.

I sit here wondering what is holding us back from being what we have always meant to be, and why is it I have heard so many times it has to be this way for now. My mind cannot handle the same old reasoning over and over again. Do you realize at all of my pain that I am to suffer as I sit here and wait for the unknown?

Why are two people made to live apart when it is apparent they share the same heart, dream the same dreams and could be no more alike? Once again I am to sit here waiting for the unknown...

Rivers Peace

She sits just beyond the river bank listening to the waters as they break from shore, she is mesmerized by the sweet comfort she feels just by being so close to the water.

She leans back on her hands feeling the breeze as it softly tickles her hair against her neck and flutter across her body, almost as if it is whispering endearments to her as she rests by the shore.

She watches as the fish jump in and out of the water in amazement at how easily it seems for them to fight and win the battle of the currents that seem to try and hold them back from finding the destination that they seek.

She is spellbound as she watches a beaver cutting down twigs and swimming down river in hopes of building his home again that the river has taken away, she giggles as she sees him paddling his way back and forth with no worries of her by the shore.

The birds are singing softly to their babies as she feeds her young and teaches them how to take flight into the sky, knowing this could be none other than goodbye. She puts her hands beneath her head looking into the sky looking at the clouds that seem to be making pictures only for her eyes. She drifts away into a peaceful sleep, and the last thing she hears is the rivers everlasting peace.

Bye for Now

I miss you more than word's can say and I now know that the saying it gets better in time for me is just a line to be said. I think of you all day long I can hear you in every song, when I lay down to go to sleep I cannot help but to weep. I see your eyes in my sleep the way they would sparkle when you would speak.

I laugh when I think of you biting your bottom lip knowing that any minute you would get whatever it was you were trying to get. I can still see your mocking face as you would look up at me with those glittering eyes making your lip's say shooooo and I would giggle wondering hmmmm what did I do.

I remember every word we said on our long nights of dreaming of one day us being together and how much we knew this felt so right. There were plenty of nights we didn't have to say a word just as long as we knew the other was there, and how we would finish each other's story's or keeping a funny one going on way to long and how we always had to share a meaningful song.

I think of all the nights we could feel each other it seemed even behind a computer screen, and to this day I still cannot figure it out how you knew what I was feeling and even thinking about to.

We have had many laughs this past year but we have also shared many tear's and saying how much better we would feel if the other was near. We were like run away teenagers just trying to break through and wondering how we could make all of our dreams come true. We could talk for hours on end and never run out of things to say and to hear your voice would always brighten my day.

I will always love you that will never end and remember you saying we will always be no matter what best friends. Ilu was our three letters and i will never use them for another, you are always in my heart and a part of my soul this is something I cannot control. As we said many nights before bed it's not bye its bye for now.

Smiling Through My Tears

I smile to hide the tears in my heart trying to understand the reasons were apart. I look up at the moon shining so bright wishing for your arms to hold me on this lonesome night. I think of all the times we have shared and wonder how now you just don't care. I take a deep breath as I decide to love the ones in my life and not the one who seemed to of done nothing but lie.

Caresses of Undying Love

May her guardian angel caress her brow with the tender touch? Of her undying love that will uplift her soul in rejoice for the life that was spared at the end of her darkened tunnel. May her spirit guild bring her peace in her heart for the battles that are to come with her long road home to us and the lord kiss her hand with his healing powers that only he can give. May her family be her backbone? That only they can give with this new life she is to live.

Hourglass

Live your life like there is no tomorrow showing all around you the person you want to be seen but hiding the real you as if in concealment of what people may think if they knew the real person that hides under her cloak in despair and fear.

Live your life like there was no yesterday full of all the tears and heartache that consumed you for so long running from a shadow that seemed to always be on your heels trying to run you down and throw more obstacles in the way to bring you to your knees.

Living your life like you are being timed by a hour glass and the sand is slowly falling just waiting to speed up at the last moment right when you have finally decided to breath your life back into your lungs, the next thing you know your time is up and your life is gone.

Live your life for the here and now show everyone the person you truly are, hiding from no one, hiding under no cloak say the words you want to say never regretting the words never spoken. Live your life like there was no yesterday and tomorrow is just a maybe but not a sure thing, the hourglass is in a race and the sand has quickened its pace.

Turning the Pages

Turning the pages in an unfinished book! A book that is to only be finished when we are gone. Reading the passages that has been your life, one that only you have had to live and write. Turning the pages to so many memories, so many of them good while others you read in disbelief and sorrow.

Turning the pages one by one wishing so many things could be undone but knowing our lives are not to be understood and we would not be the person we are today if we had walked another road made of stone.

Turning the pages laughing out loud and then crying quietly to yourself in anticipation to what is next to come. Turning the chapters one by one, pages that have already been written in stone, coming to the end of what has already been and wondering to yourself how your life's book will end.

Cherishing the Seconds

The sun shines down on such a radiating smile that makes the blue of the sky match the sparkling blue of his eyes, a smile that reaches all the way to his heart that can be seen a mile away through his baby blues.

A soft caress, a gently lingering tickle that brings smile to my face and a giggle to my lips that he then softly kisses until I melt to his body wanting to taste more of his sweetness. Loving the feel of this closeness again realizing everything I had been missing even more than I had already known.

A childish joke to be shared together making me feel like a free sprite that I had lost so long ago. A flirt that makes me blush but remembering the woman I had once been. Cherishing every second that we spend cuddled up together laughing, talking and enjoying all of these things with my friend.

Turning Back Time

Turning back time to days that were so carefree running through the gardens of flowers brings back many memories, of laughter and a youth that has long ago went away. Remembering all the times I wished to be free, not understanding that I was as free as I would ever be. Growing up was all that I wanted to be my own boss, not being told what was right or wrong.

I sit back and wonder where the time has gone and just wonder why I wanted to be grown. Wishing I knew then what I know now wishing for so many things that I can't change now. I listen to my babies tell me if they were grown they could do as they please on their own, trying to make them see it is not at all as it seems that life as a grown up is not easy.

Turning back time to my carefree days wondering where the time has went in a daze. Dreaming of all that I thought life would be not realizing just maybe I should of listened to my elders and all they said to me.

No One is Perfect

You look for Mr. Right the perfect man, why?
Are you perfect?
Do you do all you should?
You look for Miss Perfect, innocent and pure!
Why?

Are you innocent?
Do you do no wrong?

You make excuses to the bad you have suffered blaming everyone around you, why?
Could you not of done something to change your ways in this life,
did it all revolve around the other man or woman?

There is no perfect person not other than the one far away that we will all meet in our own due time.

No one has to be perfect it is not a rule that we have to bide around,
being perfect to the best of your ability is all that is and should be expected from you because no one can be perfect, even if we tried to our Heart's desire!

But you can be the perfect one to someone and that is what life is all about!!!

I am not perfect!
You are not perfect!
But together, we are perfect!!

Storybook Tales

She clutches her baby to her chest scurrying through the forest that is full of so many unwanted predators that could put a end to all of her misery in one striking moment. She is running from the life she has lived for so many years she has lost count now. She refuses to let her child live with the cruelty she has endured for so long, it is time to take her life into a different direction before it is too late for her. She has hidden under a cloak for so long that she could not even recognize herself anymore and hid from all around her.

She wonders to herself is there truly a prince out there for her like the ones her mom had read to her from the storybooks when she was wistful child living in a fantasy world? How had her life gotten so unbearable? Why had she taken the wrong turn in trusting a man she had felt from the beginning was a demon under his smiling face?

She is running toward a new life for herself and child and cares not of what may happen to them and where this road will lead; anywhere has to be better than the one she has just escaped. She dreams of a life full of heartbeats and smiling faces that are true to the eye and soul. She scurries faster now running from the darkened forest running for all she can feel a lightness come over her body as she quickens her pace now. She already feels like a weight is being lifted from her shoulders and kisses her child with tenderness that only she can give.

In a start she wakens to arms around her and can smell the blossoms of the cherry trees that line her gardens and smiles to herself as she realizes her fairy-tale has come true long ago and the woman running in the forest had been her mother saving her from a life of heartache and unbearable doom. Her heart slows to an even pace now as she turns over looking at her prince charming and thanking the woman whom she had never meant before, but in her dreams...

Bathsheba Dailey

All I Ever Need

Fingertip traces slowly lingering down my body,
as he gently outlines me with his tender touch,
leaving me with the wanting of so much more pleasures,
making me ache and asking for so much more than he has
already bestowed upon me.

Wanting glances shining from his eyes telling me he feels
the same pleasures underneath his cool and calm disguise.
I can feel his heart as it beats wildly against my skin,
a longing that we both desire to feel over and over, again.

My legs shake from the mere thought of being held in his
arms,
as he takes his fingers tracing them around to the back of
my neck leaving a shiver wherever they may roam.
I melt against his body feeling his heat against mine,
so many feelings we share cannot be denied.

Loving words being whispered into my ear
as he puts his heart and says,
there was never anything to fear,
for you have always been right here.
As the tears started to trickle down my face,
I knew right then in my heart he was here to stay
for his tender touches and loving words
are all that I shall ever need.

Breaking Down

You sit and think I will always break at your memory; you sit and think I will wait my life away, waiting for all the dreams we had planned and made. You know my soul belongs to you and only you, you believe that my heart shall wait, wait for you and all that I felt was at stake, but time has passed and my heart grows weary, waiting for someone whom really doesn't know me.

You believe I will be here waiting for the dreams and love we shared, but my life is one of lonesomeness and dread to the heartache that keeps me from wanting to get out of my bed. Sometimes my body craves your touch so much I just want to lie down and play dead as I wait for you and all that you said. I am here and you are not, and now my mind dreams of you no longer at all. My soul still yearns for you and all of our dreams and I still believe we are a love that would have always been true, but I am weary and heartbroken and no longer can wait for you. My life shall go on just as the days shall always break dawn.

Wasted Years

Please don't tell me your heart is content, was I not the one whom heard your cries as you talked of so many wasted years? Please don't tell me you are happy, was I not the one whom you told of darkened days and nights of being in a crowded room but yet so alone?

Please don't tell me that the time is not right, am I not the one whom you told that if you want something you have to chase it or lose all sight of it?

Please don't tell me you have to suffer a life of heartache to make others happy, was I not the one whom you told to live life to the fullest before my time was over and happiness would never come?

Our lives are not ones to be wasted with content heart when it can be filled with everlasting love and dreams that we will always hold dear to our hearts.

Our lives are not ones to sit in a crowded room and still feel alone when we could sit in a room with just one person and feel like our hearts are overflowing with the joy of knowing we are truly wanted and loved.

We are not supposed to live a life of unhappiness to please all those around us because if they loved us they would understand our hearts desire.

The time is right and the time has come to live our lives with that special one. Don't cry for more years wasted on a life you feel like you want to erase...

The Picture

Inflicted pain on this heart of mine reminds me of all the miles we share apart, traces of shadows still lingering in the corners reminding me of what was lost between us.

A single teardrop falls from my eye as I look at the picture that is still placed on my desk, you are still the strength that binds me to living such a life that I sometimes cannot help but to detest, but yet other times I can see all that I have and feel so very blessed.

In my heartache I can now see so much more clearly that you have and always will be here for me. As I take baby steps back into my life I look once again at the picture on my desk and smile a smile that has never been so bright. I know that one day we will have the dreams that we made but until then I am the only one that can save me..

Binding Threads

Binding threads keeping small no nonsense things together. Clothing that can be replaced or a quilt that you remember not the name behind the story of the beauty you hold in your hands but yet have cherished and handed down for generations to your loved ones.

Binding threads that hold things together means not as much as binding threads that hold the union of friendship and families together, this is something that eludes us as the time goes by and memories of what once was drifts off into the back of our minds not remembering the times we have had and the feelings of wonder that filled our hearts.

Binding threads slowly wearing down until there is nothing left but a glimmer of thread that has grown so thin it tears away from the surface leaving all that it held together falling to the earth in a unforgotten heap of lost memories.

Bathsheba Dailey

Sun Rays

Touch of sun rays sparkling in the water making for a day of great romance. Picnic basket lay on the grass not being touched, for it is all but forgotten in your sweet embrace.

The sun is falling behind the trees as it wants to rest for the night leaving beautiful colors in the sky. The moon is making way to meet the stars that are glittering the sky; they seem to be blinking just for us.

A coolness touching our bodies as it leaves the water, you wrap me tight in your powerful arms warming my skin from the nights lingering chill. A light kiss to my lips that I can barely feel but the taste of it leaves me now with a warming thrill.

We sit hours by the sparkling water, laying on our backs no need for a blanket as my head rest on your shoulder. We now watch as the moon and stars retreat behind the trees once again making way for the sun and its ever loving summer beams, hitting the water now as we fall into a peaceful sleep.

Midnight Whispering Moon

Midnight whispering moon hesitant to darken the sky with its brilliant colors and stars that over shadow the earth at the peak of nightfall. Twinkling stars waiting for their turn to brighten the sky in anticipation for wishes to be made upon them.

Night owls fluffing out their wings giving us a song letting us know they are now awake. Sleeping peacefully in our lovers arms as the moon whispers its safe keep until the day breaks light.

Midnight whispering moon hesitant to go away, now watching as the sun makes its way to brighten the sky with a new day. The moon has now left the sun to do its work as the owl sleeps and the songs of love hums from the birds are heard.

Waking to the sun that shines through the window panes, still wrapped in our lovers arms that through the night had kept us safe.

Surrendering My Trust

Surrendering my kisses to your perfect lips is so easily to do.
Surrendering my body to your sweet embrace, there is
nothing I would rather do.

Surrendering my hopes and dreams to you gives me all the
joys and pleasures in this world. Surrendering my mind to
yours is something that you can just do, knowing me so
fully and through and through.

Surrendering my soul to yours fills me up with a love I could
find nowhere else. Surrendering my trust is something that
I cannot do, for that has been broken so many times over
and over and my heart worries of the hurt it will receive.

I worry that once again my heart will fall for sweet nothing
words and once again be deceived in your loving embrace.

Falling Tears

Tears falling from my eyes hitting my face, sounds of my cries being heard only to my ears as I ponder why life has betrayed me so! My heart whimpers for the one that I hold so dear as my soul beckons for me to rest so she can feel him close to her, making sure she sheds no tears, while they are together she can be at peace.

Tears falling from my eyes as I gulp in what's left of my air, crying until I can shed not another tear! Heartbreaking songs playing on my radio, remembering the times you held me so close. I cannot bare heartbreak as this feeling as if my life's strength has been swallowed in swirling obis. Searching for you in my dreams that are the only place I see your loving grace.

Tears falling from my eyes, o how I wish to wilt away as the flowers do on the cold fall days. How I wish that I could wake from this dream and see you lying in the bed next to me. Tears falling from my eyes, feeling nothing but pain as I walk away!

Childhood Wonders

Mud puddles under their feet, splashing like a child
enjoying the games the rain have brought for them to play.
Walking a distance hearing a sound, wondering what that
could be as they walk to it to see. Seeing the squirrels
racing up and down the trees as if in a game of tag, saying
you can't catch me! Giggling as they walk away looking for
more to see on such a wondrous day!

Children singing as they jump their ropes, no worries on
their minds as they set out to play. Darkness has fallen and
the lightning bugs start to glow, chasing them, holding
them in tiny hands just to see them flashing their lights
wanting to escape and fly away. Sitting by a campfire
roasting smores, begging to stay up just a little later, and
just one more marshmallow before we have to go indoors.
Snuggled tight in the bed remembering the day that has
just past and all the days ahead.

You Know the Place

As the tears roll down her face she told him if ever he needed her he knew the place. Her heart was breaking for the man she thought had cared and had wondered why he was never there. She was all and more he had ever asked for and the feeling of knowing she was only his whore had crushed her blind and torn her heart.

She could not but wonder what all her pain had been for. She sits by her bed and wonders when she will ever feel the relief of slumber. To have loved someone so very much that all she craves is his tender touch was more than she could bare. The past is one to be left behind and the future is one she cannot decide.

She sits and wonders how she could of been so naive and what had she done to deserve such grief. The past was to stay where it was but it seems to haunt her with the light of dawn. As the tears roll down her face she still whispers you know the place.

If i am ever needed please don't hesitate, my love for you is written in the stars and on the way to whatever shall be our fate!

Heaven and Back

That old chair sits in a darkened room, to never be sit on again and to never be tossed away. Memories of love flood my body in remembrance of the love making we shared on that old brown chair. Hiding away in that darkened room!

Leaving our bodies to sit in the chair as our souls floated to Heaven entwined with each other, not aware of anyone else. No words needed to be spoken, no quite glances needed to be shared. Souls and minds talking to each other in a loving union that could be shared with no other!

Peacefully giving all that could be gave to one and another, to Heaven and back is where we drifted and hovered. Floating back to that old brown chair, giving each other glances of knowing what we had just shared. Feelings and fulfillment's that words could never say, and our hearts and souls are the only ones who know the way back to that wondrous place.

Dissipating Love

Trampling through a swirling wind! Please let me be, I have no more to give. My demise is coming from your very own hands, stop please with all of your lies and would be dreams. Give me time to spread my wings, taking enough from me have you not my sweet?

Souls searching not to find their mate, my love for you seems to only dissipate! Your memories I shall want no more....Lies in your heart to be told, leaves me trembling and obscure. Go away from me I plead of you, leave my heart won't you please. Tell me no more unless your heart is true, I wish to feel no more from you, giving my life is all I could do. So tired of searching and asking for what may be, so tired of looking to you trying to find me.

Tell me now for I will no longer wait! Tell me before all my love for you shall dissipate into the blue. I am running away from you, my heart takes beats that leaves me breathless. It wants something real and true. My soul shall have to wait and see what yours shall do. Give me reason to not take flight, give me reasons to wait for you on these lonely nights.

Tell me now for it is almost too late, my love for you continues to dissipate.

A Kiss to Your Lips

If our souls should ever meet, they would crave no one else
for all of eternity, you would see!

If you could feel the beats my heart takes, beating for
you only, make no mistake only you I can love.

If you would reach out your hand, I would grab hold
wanting no other man, when will you understand?

If you would look into my eyes, and see the love they try
to hide, you would know only for you do they cry.

If you could feel the heat that my blood boils, you would
know the passion I
feel for you leaves me weak in my knees, knowing only you
can please me.

If a kiss could say just how I love you, my lips would be
on yours forever! Never to part your sweet taste never to
leave you alone in this place!

If you would just give me this chance, I would show you
that you would never regret being my man...

Too Late to Love Me

I felt the flight like I was on angels wings; I had loved you from our very beginning. In our time together I shared all my heart with you, but you had none to spare for me, and that is why I grew apart from you. You took me for granted and hurt me so; nothing I could do would make you really whole.

I gave you chances and I gave you breaks, just trying to make our marriage one that could never break. I pleaded and I cried, walked around with black eyes, telling everyone around me unbelievable lies. Just trying to hide under a happily disguise, wanting no one to hate you, but yet in my heart I had tried.

I wanted it to last never wanting our marriage to end, never believing one day you would no longer sleep in my bed. To tell the truth as hard as it is to say sometimes I miss you even though my love for you has finally and completely faded away. I tried to make it work, not wanting to give our girls reasons to hurt.

I had no more room to bend, no more tears to cry! In the end it was just time to say goodbye! Tomorrow will be a year since the judge set me free, how sad it is to know that you now love me, the way it should have always been.

Bathsheba Dailey

Wasted Embraces

Breath your life into me for mine is slowly leaving my body every day that we are apart, show me what a happily ever ending story is really about.

Make me believe that fairy tales are not a hoax, bring me closer into your arms and hug me so tight I will never be willing to leave your side.

Kiss me with your sweet kisses; make sure I will never leave for I would never want to miss this. In your embrace, tasting such a sweet taste, us being apart is such a waste....

Lessons of the Heart

How I shudder at the thought of you, I cannot get it out of my head all the hurt you put me through! Endless games, no prize to be won but a broken heart to be looked upon. Fancy treasures are where you will stay to never understand what true love really means.

A time will come when you finally understand what it could have been to be my one and only man, but when that time comes it will be too late because my heart has finally made a long awaited escape. To be played no longer like a fiddle in the band, I have come to realize my heart can love another man.

I hear that song, you know the one! No longer do I have tears running from my eyes, no longer do I wish for my demise! I can listen to it remembering what it meant to us, I can maybe even let off steam just to vent but my heart no longer cares of the reasons it was sent. To be played can be left for someone new because my heart is now looking for something true. I can love you until the days are nothing more than old memories. But that is just what they are, old memories between me and you.

Hidden Tears of a Man

Teardrops fall from his eyes, a wet cheek he covers to hide. He is a man and men never cry! Tormented things always on his mind! A soft melody plays in the room, his daydreams start to roam.

He dreams of things he cannot have, at times feeling like his heart can turn to ash. He sits in a darkened room all alone, his heart every second turning to stone. Life has turned its back on him, feeling as if he has not one friend. Life not giving him a chance to dream, unfulfilled dreams it always seemed!

All he wants is a love that truly rings lifting his heart and soul through firing rings. A melody plays in his darkened room as once again tears linger in his eyes, and he tells himself life is nothing but unforgivable lies...

True Love and Soul Mates

We look for the one who we think could be our soul mate not realizing that is not so easily to come by, not realizing for most we miss each other on the way of living our lives. We find what we believe is our true love and put into place they are our true mate that has been out there just waiting for us to find. I believed they were one and the same, true love and soul mates.

My belief has now changed for to ever be with my soul mate will only happen when I leave this place called earth that I am traveling in. I am learning the world; it is just getting better in time until I am given a leave to be with him in a world much more divine.

True love we can find here on earth, he can be mine. To cherish for all days to come until our time on earth has run low. To be placed beside each other for all time we will stay, once we have died and gone away.

What happens then when we go away? Do we linger on with our true love or our soul mate? Soul mates we feel to never have meant, only knowing he is our own when passing by. Feeling a hold on our bodies and searching their knowing eyes. Our bodies release sparks of fire, tears in our eyes knowing togetherness right now we cannot find.

I have meant my true love never to hold until the end of my life, to me this seems so unfair, never to feel right!

I believe I know now who my soul mate is, never to of meant, tears run from my eyes as I think of him and wonder why togetherness we cannot find.

I take steps in a new direction believing god will lead the way, believing one day to be with my soul mate

Hearts and Souls

A Powerful Love to Miss

Tell me how it is; stop making our love one to miss. I need you like the sun needs day, tired of crying at the mere thought of our loving days.

Take me in your arms with a roughness that says we do belong together and as I have always known forever.

Kiss my lips with yours; I miss your sweet taste like the night would miss the stars that grace the sky.

Let me wake up beside you in the morning where every day our love seems new and every kiss is one to die for.

Don't you miss my sweet kisses to? Intertwine your body with mine, legs wrapped together making love to each other.

Another as great we will never find. Peacefulness coming from your powerful arms, calmness comes over me, one that only you can show me. Let me taste your sweet kisses let it be your embrace that I will never have to miss.

Sandy Shores

White sandy shores, tickling my toes with its grain!

Seagulls flying overhead looking for its next meal to take. Water rushing in with the tide hitting my legs, it is cool and mild. The smell of salt lingering in the air, giving me total glee to feel such peace. Watching children learn their first swim, building castles with sand.

Seashells scattered all around, looking for the ones that makes beautiful watery sounds. All kinds of magical colors can be seen now, as the sun falls on the oceans tide mirroring itself. Couples walking hand in hand as they tickle their toes in the sand, loving chatters to one another as they watch the waters flow back out again.

A Love Never to be Defined

I remember everything you ever said to me! My heart cannot breath it is in such disbelief. I fear I will never feel for another as I do you, our love was one that we waited for many a years. I try to say goodbye to you, but the tears fall just from the thought of loving anyone but you. I try so hard to move on, but it never fails thoughts of you are brought on or the melody of our favorite songs plays in my heart you have always stayed.

I try to understand why things worked out the way they did, knowing you as no other could. I knew you were just in love with me as I you. Why stay in a hopeless life? Why do all you said you would not? why live as a half of a person? Knowing with me you could of been whole. I try to think I had been played but I know that is not so, your kisses told me what was the truth, I miss them but not as much as you.

I try to move on; I try to laugh I even fake I can love again but in my heart there could never be another as you.. One of a kind someone true in my dreams that could only be you. A true love never to be found again, waiting for you to comprehend. I can feel you in my heart, I know when life is at it's harshest, I feel when you feel life is nothing more but hopeless. A love like that can never be defined, a love like that use to be mine.

Bathsheba Dailey

Far Away Friends

Trumpets play as the sun sets, beautiful colors lighting up the sky.

People dance and people cry for the beauty is more than meets the eye. All kinds have gathered in one place, no one caring of the others race, sharing words from each other's hearts, loving all that we truly are.

Understanding we all are the same, no matter how far away we may be. Hearing so much on the news, not understanding why so many feuds! We walk this earth torn apart, by other mans greed and hardened hearts.

To be united would be a blessing, for everyone to just stop all the fussing. My friends are worth so much more than fought-en over oil. To fight over something so cold and black not worrying of the hot red blood that is spilled.

My heart cries out for so many lost in this war, and look to my far away friends as my heart cries out feeling torn. So to my far away friends no this to be true you have a true friend with a heart that is full of love for you.

I know in our hearts we all are the same, no one better and each other not to blame....

Heaven Sent

Heaven sent, tranquility sets in for the first time I am not hidden inside with tremors. Trust in you as I have not often done, feeling like we are truly happy as one.

Peaceful moments shared together, my lovers embrace I long to feel against my skin! Missing you when you are away, longing to see your beautiful face. Shimmering lights flickering from your eyes, what he wants not being disguised.

A truce made to give into each other's needs, only being together can we fulfill and please. Arms and hands racing to feel the other, loving the taste and pleasures we can always discover in the arms of the other.

Heat rises from our bodies, temperatures flare from your every touch. Give each other what we need only together can our hearts and bodies be completely pleased.

Faking a Life to Live

I do not care what keeps you there, to live your life as a fake making yet again another mistake. This I can bear no more, this made up world that is only yours. Shadows hide in the corners of the house, not to understand what brings your heartaches about.

A sweet song to be heard a mile away makes you think of a long time wait. Fearing yourself to take control, showing the entire world who you really are. Waiting for death to take you away, waiting for the time you can be free.

Sitting alone watching the shadows in the corner, sitting alone having nothing to look forward to any longer. Taken breaths in just trying to make another day go by, trying to make everyone believe your who you say you are upon built up lies that have gone too far. Can you make the true one believe or can they see your hiding yourself in grief.

A deceitful life is one to be lived, not to others but one far worse. A deceit that hides within, not knowing who truly you can depend. A great man hides behind his beautiful heart, one day to leave this world wondering what had kept him hiding as a shadow in the corner always feeling so torn apart.

Open your eyes and see what is right in front you before it is too late and in a corner you shall always wait.

True Hearts

He walks in and out of her life, how can this be right?
Knowing he is all that she needs, knowing he is the only
one who can make her heart bleed.

Not meaning to give her distress but not yet realizing
the life he has forgotten and left. Her heart cries out to
make him see his everlasting love is all that she would ever
need to stay alive and breathe.

An angel to her he seems a touch to her face so gently can
make her weak to her knees. A love like his being her
saving grace with just that tender touch to her face.

To no longer love him would mean to not have a heart any
longer, but to stay only seems to tare her heart apart
more every day. Her heart has been deceived, her eyes
to blind to see the truth that only her mind could see, he
was not one to be believed.

His dreams he was too scared to follow through with, to
weak to achieve what his heart told him to do. To scared
and frightened to be with the one who could of been his
everything, to scared his heart would be left crushed only to
bleed with his undying love and every need.

A love to be fought for a love that is so true, a love that
would make you see my love for you is real and could never
die. Darkness keeps our love apart making us never be with
the one who truly holds our hearts.

Tell Me Anything

Push me down to the ground make me believe you are not what I need. Tell me I am everything as you once again walk out the door leaving me to cry and feeling once again I had been deceived.

Make my eyes swollen with the tears that I cry, tell me everything you ever said to me was nothing short but regretful lies. Tell me all that needs to be said trying to turn me against you with dread.

Push me down to the ground; hurt me as much as you can. Tell me you are not all that I ever wanted in love and from a man. Trick me with your hateful words make me feel that love can only hurt. Tell me to find another tell me that our dreams cannot be seen any longer.

Make me believe this is what you need me to do, no longer wanting to give me hurt that can only come from you.

Tell me anything you want me to believe, tell me I had only been deceived. Tell me your heart and body does not cry out for mine, but always know I can tell when you are lying.

Today is Tomorrow

Always wrong never right, tired of the same old heartbreaking fight! I know what to do not liking it any better than you. Trying to wait for what was to be, hesitant now because nothing has changed as far as I can see. Follow through with what I should do, would be so much easier if I were not so in love with you.

Always wrong never right, I did not make this choice, my heart had done as you're told it to do. Too much pain, too much sorrow, so tired of waiting for tomorrow! Telling me that I am not all that I should be, give me guilt for what you conceived. Telling me all will be as should be, if I would only wait for you until another day.

Too much pain too much sorrow, today is tomorrow!!

Tear Drops

I am so tired of hurting; feeling like my beating heart has been ripped from chest. Tears spilling on my already soaked pillow, dreams of you that never go away. To be teased with your love when you have memories of us! Then out of my life again you go puff, I cannot take anymore teasing of us, my heart is not that tough and my tears are drowning me in my sleep.

To look back at a life that you always promised you would make right just to hurt me more than I have ever been in my life keeps me at bay not living my life to the fullest not wanting to be hurt again, not wanting to feel again at least then there would be no tears to shed when I lay in my bed with memories of what could of been.

I play a fools game believing everything you say, believing that in time we will be once again more than just loving friends. I walk a road of heartache and pain waiting out the waiting game, not even sure if both sides are being played, or am I just part of a hopeless game. I sit by this stream as the tears fall from my eyes, screaming a thousand hurtful good byes. Ready to give up, ready to take flight, ready to just try and get on with my life. But no matter how many tears I have cried and how many times I have tried to walk away my mind once again starts to stray remembering the love we had and all of our beautiful memories. How do you give up on such a love one that you know was made just for us?

I write these words from my heart trying to figure it out
wonder why we are still apart. I know that your love has
not subsided! I can feel your heart with mine as they both
cry out for what they know should be, but they have to live
without. How can you linger in a world that you do not
belong?

Do you not remember the words we said and felt for so
very long?

Do you not remember our hearts beating as one as
you held me tightly dancing to a beautiful love song?

I go to bed now as the tears are already fallen from my
eyes, wishing to hold you as our bodies, hearts and souls
take a trip into the beautiful night sky. Going to faraway
places that were only meant for you and me!

Tired

Tired of it all, ready to go to a place that pain is not heard of! I cannot take this life of struggles anymore, never any peace to be had! Just gloomy days to be seen ahead of me! So much drama, so many lies all I want to do is go under a cloak and hide from my life.

People walking around smiles on their faces, wish I knew what the smiles were for. Never ending it seems this life I lead, to many people give me reasons to leave. Stomach in knots feeling like it could explode, Do I want to leave this earth or just get up and move? What do I need to prove anymore? Nothing matters at all I just wish I could take a tumble out of this life I want to fall. Dealing with heartache that never goes away, a man who told me I was all he would ever need. Another man who won't go away, tired of seeing his drunk ass face, wish he would once again just go away.

Hands shake and the tears start to roll, frustration is taking its toll on me, God I just want to leave. When will it ever end? When will life just please end.

Unseen Hearts

Screaming, pleading feels like my heart has stopped all beating. Crying and dying inside so many lies have got me down and making me wish for a place to hide. Head hurts, chest hearts more than anything my heart hurts... Tired of the one's I love out to desert me, not realizing I would be anything that they needed. Sweet memories, loving embraces nothing more now than lies told to my face. Hiding inside of myself not wanting to be seen, to love people just causes me unwanted pain.

Invisible shield to hide myself from this world, never to leave it again... Never wanting to feel this pain and turmoil again, never will I let another see what hides beneath my heart that has yet again been ruined. I will smile in the face of those that say sweet things but trust me when I say the real me you will never see.

Forgotten memories, torn to pieces heart, I now am to live my life in the dark. Don't question me of what lies beneath, for even I cringe at the thoughts of the games that have destroyed the real me. From this day forward my heart will watch it's every beat.

Diversity

Diversity in our lives can not to be explained, wondering when the end of the world will finally come, Taking away all of our pains! Tear drops not to be heard for they are shed within; bodies that cannot let another anymore see their pain. Passages written in the stars, not understanding what it is we are supposed to see... Nothing in the sky to us but a beautiful sea of glittering lights! Days pass us by one by one, we let ourselves be hurt by those we love.

We come unfolded by the seams wishing we sometimes could be taken by the sea, engulfed by the waves that come in with the tide. Wishing for once we did not have to hide the tears in our eyes. Sitting on this lonely road to nowhere, the rain drops this time can hide my tears. The sound of thunder can be heard in my ears, and for a moment it can hide the sounds of my heartaches and fears.

I Still Believe

I still believe in soul mates I still believe in true love, my heart is still the same and no one can change that. I have been through heartaches, I have been through unbearable pain, but my heart will love again.

It may take time, it may be awhile but my heart deserves the one man that will be my whole world and be only mine. I may cry for a love lost, my heart torn to shreds like un-watered moss, but in time all my tears will dissolve like the rain the sun has shined upon.

I may wish upon a star tonight, for the love that felt so right. I may beg to god to make it right, to show me the reasons he never fought the fight. I may ask a million things and may dream a million dreams, I am an emotional mess and I won't deny this. But I am a believer of a greater love that is just waiting to be found by me.

About the Author

*B*athsheba Dailey has always loved to write poetry, wanting only later to indulge her passions to share her emotional feelings and experiences that could only be conveyed through the proper medium of ink, pen and paper. She has three beautiful girls who are the inspirational world in which she thrives. A single mom living in West Virginia most of her life, Bathsheba currently now engages work at a local restaurant and going to school to better the lives of herself and her three children.

www.ingramcontent.com/pod-product-compliance
Lightning Source LLC
Chambersburg PA
CBHW060444040426
42331CB00044B/2605